Horse Logic

Poems by Terry Persun

Cyberwit.net

HIG 45 Kaushambi Kunj, Kalindipuram
Allahabad - 211011 (U.P.) India
http://www.cyberwit.net
Tel: +(91) 9415091004
E-mail: info@cyberwit.net

Copyright© Terry Persun
ISBN: 978-93-88319-74-4

First Edition: 2021
Rs. 200/-

Printed at Thomson Press India Limited.

For Catherine, Nicole, and Joe,

who completely understand

ACKNOWLEDGEMENTS

Previously published in literary magazines, sometimes in a different form:

"A Long Sleep" — *1ˢᵗ and Hope*

"Bridge" — *Minotaur*

"Horse Lessons" — *Minotaur*

"In the Midwest" — *Parting Gifts*

"Night Feeding" — *Ramblr*

"Only So Far" — *Rag Mag*

"Poor Farmers" — *Cirque*

"Waking Up" — *Main Street Rag*

Previously published in collections, sometimes in a different form:

"An Unnatural Path" — *Balancing Act*

"Broken" — *Sentences*

"Coop" — *Sentences*

"Dolly" — *Navigating Wind*

"Everyday Returns" — *Broken Fingers*

"Farming" — *Sentences*

"Feeding" — *Every Leaf*

"Fence Line" — *Sentences*

"Fingers" — *Sentences*

"Full" — *Balancing Act*

"Hands of Man" — *Plant-Animal-I*

"Horse Poem" — *Every Leaf*

"Little Celebrations" — *Every Leaf*

"My Sister's Heart Attack" — *And Now This*

"On Leaving" — *And Now This*

"Storm" — *Sentences*

"The History of It" — *Plant-Animal-I*

"Trespassing" — *Every Leaf*

Contents

Day Farmer

An Unnatural Path

Through the openings between trees
in the forest, there is an unnatural path
which leads to a wide pond
placed at the edge of a hay field

near a wood frame house and barn.
The flat black of water reflects
a bird infested sky.

Near the edge, the pond scum separates
and the silver bellies of minnows wink.
Tadpoles slip near the green of a stem
and dream of having legs.

Concrete

In college we're taught
to use specific, concrete images
when writing poems as heavy as stone,
yet in lit class
we learn the weight of words
that drag time behind them

like an old potato sack.
But when I use words
like "cow" or "fence"

they do not seem to be so weighted down
by image or time,
no stone, no potato sack,
just a barbed wire fence,
rusted and sagging,
keeping in the Guernseys,
or keeping me out
of a wide field of tall oat grass
I could easily say
is my own freedom.

Bridge

I built a bridge
of owl feathers
across Chimacum Creek
into eight acres
of failing hay fields
until I realized
that the barred owl
had come for me

not the land I believed
called my name.
A turn in dream began
years after my soul
had eaten so much pain,
that my body couldn't see
clearly enough to know
it had already changed.

The true bridge built
was not of feathers,
but words that couldn't
arrive any other way
but to be squeezed
from the thin tube I became
once I selected the side path
I was meant to take.

barbed wire fence
    tightrope
            for hanging roses

Rain

The sky became heavy.
Like worms from the clouds,
it rained long strips
of perfect wetness
onto the gray-white sidewalk.
Inside the houses, lights

went on, music played.
People began to dance.
It was the farmers
who needed the rain.
Without fully understanding why,
those in the city contributed

to the joy through movements
of their own interpretation.
Like a chain tied
to a swinging bucket,
their hearts lifted
and they didn't even know why.

Waking Up

It is as quiet as deer tracks.
When the rooster crows, it hurts.
Even ravens are startled.
Swans paint the sky in honks.
Multiply birds times silence.
Fog listens to the air breathe.

Crickets gather the dark.
Insects creep from thin air.
The earth waits for feet.
Families sleep late.
Grass rises to meet summer.
Sway to the sound of wind.

Hear the hollow sounds of cows.
How much longer will it be?
The sun plays the treetops.
Vision opens to new dreams.
It is time to begin.
Walk early in coyote sunlight.

Little Celebrations

—for Ted Kooser

It is good to learn
the habits of birds
and the smell of fescue
growing in the side field.
Mornings secretly rise
above the fog-like river
along the valley floor.
Peeking around

the corner of the barn
at five a.m. reminds
me of the little celebrations
that nature hands us
throughout the busy day,
the celebrations we ignore
even as we head toward
the end of our own
long walk from home.

Snake

Its red stripe scrapes
against the stick of my leg.

Surprised by movement,
each step is now tentative.

The snake is more frightened
than I am, but knows

its own long life,
which frightens me.

Hands of Man

From the hilltop, the morning's mist
lies like cotton over the trees.
The old truck, rusted and silent,

sits lazily under a sprawling oak.
The combine beats the corn
off the stalk, silks fluttering

like light blonde hair in the wind.
The smell of cornmeal, the dust
of corn stalks, the broken silence

of the day, pull together
to join hands and dance
inside the body of the farmer

who has called up the gifts
of earth using the hands of man.

Hay Music

My arms broke the silence
of hay field with the music
of their violin string muscles

tightening as I lifted one
bale after bale after bale.
The tune of truck engine

harmonized while it waited
for me to break its idle
into orchestral motion,

the next stop opposite
three packed and strung
bales along the endless
horizon of haying season.

Fingers

They've been nailed before.
Symmetry does not recognize its twin.
Movement changes their shapes.
Shadows look nothing like them.
Ten individuals with one mission.
They say little on their own.

Fingers hold everything seriously.
They are the manipulators of the body.
Each is different from all the others.
Selection finds them grouped together.
They can become an instrument.
Feeling arrives through the tips.

Oh, what they've done.
Who could understand it all?
An entire life is drawn from them.
Roaming is their passion and job.
Expression leaps from them.
An easy life can be a hard living.

Sick

Neurology failed
the stray cat
unable to walk
or jump from the cabinet
so Dad did what
he had to do
what he had to do often
in that valley
we lived in.

Killing isn't pretty
it's necessary
to protect the other cats
or dogs or horses.
Disease jumps
the fence of species
more often
than we'd like.

The flu is evidence
that we should care
for our animal
brothers and sisters,
our whole living
family.

Ten

When I bought the farm,
there was a dump in the back

of the place. About a mile
behind the house, the land

fell away quickly. Trees had
tumbled down the hill

after a huge storm, and trash
had been thrown after.

I rented an excavator
for a few months one summer

and you just don't want to
know what I found down there.

Coop

Blood spills from smashed thumb.
Like clockwork, anger seeps out.
Little does anyone know.
Everyone has gone inside.
It's not the hammer's fault.
The project had a crack.

Standing with tools in a mob.
Hand to hand combat is real.
Insects sigh, but never rest.
The day's sweat lingers.
Deliver, deliver, deliver.
Shade settles near shoulders.

Ideas are tested twice.
Who will help when it's needed?
Twisted body holds tools.
I'm kneeling on stones.
Torso stiffens into resistance.
The chickens can't wait.

Chicken Shit

Horse shit doesn't smell
so bad after cleaning
a few chicken coops.
    The eggs are good,
    the chickens friendly,
    but, man, isn't there something
    else we could feed them?

As hot as summer gets,
the breeze isn't welcome,
    wafting with it the chicken run,
    dug-up and spread out,
    and limp with feces.

And now the state wants
more from our meager living
    and won't take eggs
    as payment, having their own
    chicken shit rules to live by.

Poor Farmers

Sweltering even in the shade
of woods near us. One deep
sigh blinks sweat from eyes,
a backhand swipe brushes hay
from cheeks. Half the wrestling team
stops to drink tepid water
from refilled milk jugs.

Earlier that day we horsed around,
threw bales over the wagon
onto a friend, but deep into afternoon light,
with rain climbing the back side
of the western ridge, there's no time
to waste. The jagged edge of youth smells

like warm mold. We know
there's a cooked meal at the blunt end
of our push through the day.
Yet we'd rather ride into town
where city girls point and laugh
as we drive past in our pickups,
running out on our lives.

Old Fences

Now a tractor path,
the road darted, crow-
straight along
the fence line,
now disintegrated

by time
and oxidation.
Pieces of barbed
wire creep
like worms

to the surface
to be noticed,
picked up,
regarded a mystery.
Giving back

to the earth
what was given
them, fence posts
rot and bear new life
where last

the wind lowered them.
A spitting rain
becomes a reminder
of the weather
that beats us all down.

Tree Growing from a Stone Fence

Each stone on the old fence
has toppled into the now unused field
as though it had once been placed there.
The oldest trees stand as part of the fence,
not as markers and not because they were planted
to separate one owner's property from another,

but for simpler reasons:
for, who would cut another's tree?
For years, decades, at town gatherings
the trees were forgotten.
No one asked: "Was that maple growing
near my corn field planted by you?"
or "Where did that grove of birches
come from that is nestled tightly
into the large corner area of four stone boundaries?"

So the old maple we came upon,
tucked between younger trees which have overtaken
the old farm, stands, not only as a monument,
but as a memory of two farmers, their sons,
and their sons, a memory
to hard work, disappointment, glory.

Like an Old Farm

We are like an old farm
in spring when the stream
runs full and the pond is deep.
Green sprouts alive and sensuous
into the crisp morning air
the wind is sweeping away
to let in summer.

Farmers are out plowing
to lay new crops for harvest.
The barn fills with sounds
of birds flying among the rafters
and of wild animals aching to get out.

Our souls are locked
like the barbed-wire fence
that once was nailed to the maple
growing at the edge of the field,
how, through years of being together,
the maple has grown around the wire,
has taken it in close to its heart
and holds tight.

Only So Far

The tractor's path
begins with such strength
of purpose, running down weeds
and hollowing out the ground.
Its tire treads visible
in the first ten yards
like giant claws scratching
the once loose dirt.

Beyond a point,
the weeds return,
reseed, shift their roots
to the side as though leaning
into a strong wind.
The tire marks become faint,
thinning into small mounds,
disappearing into the open field.

Having run their course,
the tracks give way,
happy to be included,
in some small way satisfied,
with being a part of a larger thing:
a meaning to the weeds that have learned
to begin again under different circumstances.

Day Farmer: The Horses

We Had Horses

It was easy to talk to the horse
which had become my friend.
Who in my family would listen so closely?
I could open up in the security
of barn and hay and whinny.

Even deer stood grazing
when I rode bareback near them.
I could have touched their white tails,
stroked their bony brown necks,
fed them from my hand.

Yet, during nights with a full moon,
that horse would kick and bite
at her stall doors.
She would stretch her neck
wishing to escape.

It took me years to find
that people could listen too,
that deer could be more than venison,
that no stall door could hold me.

Feeding

In the darkness
of the hallway closet
I've learned the feel
of my jacket

as I get ready
to feed the horses.
The cold air is a rock
snapped against my forehead.

Stones crunch, break loose
under my boots
and scatter.
Nickers draw me

down the slope
to hungry animals
like me, eager
for breakfast.

Hay Day

Not too early.
Nine, ten.
The equipment kicks
into gear: trucks,

tractors, rake, baler.
Already cut, the hay
waits to be rolled
over, tired in the sun,

dry on top, wet
under the ears.
In a matter of hours
the baler gobbles

the hay from the field
and pushes it into long
blocks of horse feed,
the job barely begun.

Think

What do they think,
those horses, while trapped

inside their turn-outs
encircled by electric wire

pulsing in spasms
of current, shocking

if touched. Whole lives
lived, spent, in a few

thousand square feet
of pasture. A shelter

against wind and rain.
Three squares a day,

occasional treats: carrots,
apples, pellets. I think

of being house-bound,
hospitalized, limited

to where I can go,
yet other fields, forests,

roads leading away,
are always visible, calling.

I want to follow clouds
as far as they float
and take a few horses along.

Horse Poem

How many have saved a life
or lives, and then been beaten,

sold, or destroyed?
The sun rises to lighten

their load, warm their heavy bodies.
Walking the desert puts sand

at the base of your soul.
Riding creates another bond,

even an electric storm
can't break down.

Let's say we think of our
own safety first, then

after painful extraction
from our thoughts, transferred

our care, let it accumulate
and shape-shift in the fog

of our genius, until it lands
outside our own bodies.

How would the two-headed
animal that we have become look?

Running together eliminates
the sky's need to cry out.

Seven

Numbers of.
Sites to see.
City blocks.
Step off the sky.
Drink up.
Silver slips down.
The rain drain.

Plato believed in them.
Two, five, seven.
The difference, the sum.
We've learned
to sum up,
reduce, divide,
separate.

Two parents, two brothers, one sister, me, family. Seven.
Three towns, four cities. Seven.
Once good friend, three kids, two lives, one game. Seven.
The empty sky, filled bucket, grass, three trees, one world. Seven.
It all makes numerical sense if you break it into insignificant groups.

When I was five I dreamed of seven white horses. I was
dying then. Alone. Sick and in bed. Seven white horses against
the black night sky. Eldon said I was lying about them, that they
were a hallucination because they were in the sky. I cried, but he
never let up. "I was dying," I said. "They were coming for me.
And you," I pointed, "all you could do was drag me back by my feet."

"I didn't touch you."

"By my feet," I said. "You should've let me die. I'd be riding now. Up there."

He slapped my fingers. "Yeah, I should'a let you die."

I looked at him. Stared. "You did."

It took a long time for him to admit it, admit that he did let me die, and that I wasn't alive anymore. That I wasn't real.

And then it was too late. He was gone too. "Eldon!"

I looked up and there were those horses. Seven of them coming for me. I just held out my arms.

The Sun's Roses

Their hides were red
and white and black
as the colors were meant to be.
They owned the prairie
and the hills with their wild
galloping and hoof-strike
battles for seniority.

They grew and bred,
multiplied on their own,
without help, without control,
and were strong
as nature permitted.

Before domesticated,
they bore no packs,
no riders. Pride was in knowing
the sun would rise
and the long grass
would feed them through summer.

Mixed Dream Metaphors

After departing the ferry
I turn and watch it leave
reminding me of the stock barn fire
that stopped me from getting home
one night. This time water

is in the way. No worries,
the neighbor's cats will still get fed.
As the water morphs into memory,
my first marriage looms over the head

of the artist working on his painting.
Suddenly, dad is working too, an artist
building a dam with the skill of baristas

making that millionth cup of coffee.
You'd think all this would depress me,

but I get on my horse and gallop away.

Pride

Finally, on the mend
after a recent accident
involving two cows
and a frightened horse.

Mending all those broken
bones was easy,
it was my embarrassment
when flying over those cows,
my horse with planted feet,
that unsteadied my nerves.

My mended pride
scaled my idea of failure,
mended my sense of self,
and took me for a psychological
ride my horse couldn't do.

When I think I'm an expert
at anything, the universe
always finds a way to remind me
that my expertise is only a shallow
creek running next to a raging river.

Dolly

One of the horses is mine
but I had to get married
at seventeen
and missed
our entire life together.

Horse Lessons

There's no need to escape
if there's food on the table,
no such thing as greener
unless the cupboards are bare.
Drink after meals to aid digestion.

A fence doesn't have to be tall
but must be comfortable
to be an effective home.
The people must be kind.

It's alright to be cared for,
in the most intimate ways,
as long as you give everything
when the request is made.

A Long Sleep

As if in death, he steps
through his own heart
in sleep.
The blanket's hollow sounds wrap
around his dreaming head

and fold down
and under like a hand
grasping at something it needs.
R.E.M. remembers
a future time

along some dirty highway
where his body lies
in mown grass, where
horses and antelope graze
with wolves

the color of his wife's hair.
Through a haze of moon-glow
and half-sleep, he twists
loose from the blankets
and in his dream

flies over the highway.
The wolves turn into butterflies
and the horses become
all the children
he will meet in his lifetime.

Night Farmer

Farming

Twilight, and the chickens are in.
The sky is blooming.
Fence posts creak with complaint.
Wire sings electric.
A hundred birds lift the air.
Night settles into shadow.

Coyotes remind their prey.
Noises have no faces.
Walking becomes treacherous.
People move inside the house.
The porch light goes out.
The stars are excited.

The dark oozes through alone.
How does it travel?
A breeze kicks at the leaves.
Cold tempts the night.
Nothing changes significantly.
The field sucks everything in.

moonrise
    water shifts
            its weight

New Light

The light turns auburn
as the sun sets below
the green tops of trees.
At dusk the world, the valley,
looks differently: a color shift

welcomes new life
blooming like the poisonous
tansy ragwort that grows
along the tractor path.

Deer linger
into the new light,
raccoons chatter
from high in trees, coyotes
go on the prowl.

The Cows are Birthing at Night

The moon is the midwife to black
calves that turn in their skins
searching for their dark beginnings.

The sky closes its doors
as not to scare them
from their own screams.

Like human babies born at night,
tall grass pries open to expose
the mythical animal that exists,
all fur, darkness, and friend to the moon.

In the Midwest

The city lights fade,
reach for the country,
go down the dirt road
near the cow pasture
and corn field,
next to holy roller churches,
and wish to be a sunny day
in the playground of a grade-school
lost somewhere in the midwest.

The city lights reach down
to the sidewalk strollers
who remember yesterday's satisfactions
while rubbing their hands together.
The gray-brown sidewalks sparkle,
bits of glass like eyes
watching every stroller wander
in and out of their own memories,
searching for a place to rest
somewhere in the midwest.

Bottomland

The clouds rush south
leaving empty promises
in the turned-up
leaves of apple and pear
trees, and in the exposed
backs of beetles and birds.

The Orchard Grass lies
over as if brushed
by an invisible groomer,
then straightens its silvery
stalks exposed in the bottomland.

A nymph steps out
of the darkness of stone
and scrambles along
the tractor path, frightened
by the farmer's footsteps
and the sensation of invariable rain.

Fence Line

A separation has begun.
Sides have been acknowledged.
The way is assumed straight.
Sight recognizes no difference.
Something isn't quite right.
Things exists for a reason.

Boundaries can be broken.
Witness the growing of fields.
Coyotes migrate across lines.
Hawks fly oblivious of barriers.
From a distance there's no change.
The sun blankets it all.

Stay on one side or the other.
Which way does the wind blow?
Wait for the long shadows.
Highlight what means the most.
Keep all sections apart.
Let the division mean something.

The History of It

Passing the open fields
of pasture remnants of oat
crops lift among the prickly
weeds and colorful wildflowers.
The deserted husk of an old
Farmall tractor rusts — red
against red — near the roadside
just beyond a small drainage
ditch once used to guide run-off
water into the creek down the road.

In a spark of setting sunlight,
the old farmer once again rides
the metal seat, hand throttling
the powerful red work horse forward,
then steps hard, braking the right
wheel, turning 360 degrees
without missing a heartbeat, harvesting
what was planted centuries ago.

The tires of the jeep pick up dust
from the roadside and quickly obscure
the tractor in the rearview
mirror until the mind takes over
and fills in the gaps, the history
of it still floating in the air,
still smelling of the future.

Chicken Farm

Standing next to two sisters,
I find I can not move forward
or back, not side to side.
When they push, my beak
hits its clipped and blunted
end against soft flesh.

Eggs fall from me,
the scent of it twice my own.
They are taken and kept,
or eaten.
Screams from thousands
like me ring inside
the coffin of a building
that lies to us about days
and seasons.

In seventy weeks,
I hear,
we are butchered
and sold like so many eggs.
Seventy weeks, just long enough
for madness to creep up
but not to take hold,
just long enough
for our beaks to heal
almost shut.

Trespassing

The far fence
leans toward the brown

and white cows
like a conversation.

The length of the fence
can stretch into unlikely concerns.

For instance, the fence wanders
onto the neighbor's property.

A single mistake,
a wrong glance,

a misstep. Tears shed
won't remake the bed

or rectify the barbed
wire relationship.

Storm

The wind throws leaves into the window.
Sound drops, scrapes, flies away.
Each stone hides under the weight of air.
No sky cries like this one does now.
Trees have become frightened.
Rabbits hide in yellow bushes.

Chairs, in this room, are warmed by sun.
Nothing lasts like misused happiness.
Starlings struggle to return to their nests.
People strain to hear the lecture.
Words are dropped from the ceiling.
Rain darts penetrate the skin.

Listening stretches thin.
What is true obligation?
Stars are always out, always.
Someone grips their aura and pulls it in.
Ravaged chickens love the coyote.
Sleep comes noisily these days.

Howling Dogs

The hollow wail of hounds
in the dark of night
beyond the thin walls
of the bedroom frighten

the whole household
because each of them
knows that the superstition

that hounds barking
at night means a death
to someone close
is about to come true.

Another Night

Quick with the ax or machete,
cut clean, the chicken's neck,
body thrown into the play-yard
to stumble blindly until death
runs it down and tackles.

The smell of hot water soaking
wet feathers cannot be forgotten,
plucked and scraped, bare where
only ten minutes before, alive.

The choice at dinner clear,
remember the clucking or plucking,
or forget altogether. "Don't stare,
eat," my dad would say, "or go
to bed hungry," another night.

On Leaving

I stand in the middle
of the hay field
as it leans one way,
and on a windless morning
shifts miraculously,
like a school of fish,
in a new direction.

The tall grass and I live
among invisible winds —
or some other miracle —
that leans against me until
the fish carry my heart
in a new direction.
All my life

people, circumstances, responsibility.

At the closing of the day,
the sun brightens everything
it touches, and it touches
me. Backlit as though I am
a holy man, I spread
my arms to accept
the dawn, the golden light
spreading out as far
as I can see, drawing the best
out of everything it touches,
everything it can't touch.

Night Farmer: The Horses

Everyday Returns

Mosquitos gather around
the horses in early evening.

Swallows have them nervous
about the thinness of air.

Clouds play games with the light
around the barn and haystack.

My quiet time spins memory
from familiar to mystery

like a handful of walnuts
dropped from a nearby tree.

Nothing is ever exactly the same
when I return for a feeding.

It's as though the universe
doesn't even know I'm here.

Many Places

Every sky-bright evening
she walks to leased property
and seven waiting horses
to wash together a mash
of pellets, vitamins, and rice
bran meant to keep them healthy
until each chooses to die—
in its own *good* time.

Silence becomes orange sound,
creeks of trees, the cat's patter,
maybe bird or bat wings.

Home can be many places:
a barn or pasture, a beach,
inside your own heart.

Morning happens a million
times, never twice the same,
yet love and life, clichéd
as they are, stretch beyond
it all—all the way to becoming
who you really are.

Night Feeding

I worry for Shane's feet.
His hooves are tender
on the hard surface
of frozen mud. He acts lame
for the night, while his mini friend,
Vanna, trots toward the hay
I just put down.

Next are the chickens,
all in their coops except one.
Roo is wild and it must be
completely dark or I can't
catch him. But in the dark
he's docile. I pick him up
like a child's balloon,
and place his delicate body
into his coop for the night,
so raccoons and birds of prey
can't reach him.

Finally, the other horses—my wife
has fed her fair share by now—
we feed together, talking
of stars, darkness, and night birds,
like the barred owl we once saw
sitting on the wheelbarrow handle
when we arrived. Satisfied
the animals are alright, we're back
in the warm truck, eager for home,
to warm each other in bed.

My Sister's Heart Attack

Ponies live a long time
if cared for, and Nosey
got brushed daily, fed
grain and clean hay

for all the years my sister
lived at home. Marriage stole
her away, but Nosey stayed
and, like the rest of the herd,

became too much for Mom.
Nosey lived on though, pastured
in a side field that flooded
once a year, overflowing

the tires we stuffed rocks into
to make a water barrier. She grazed
through my sister's divorce,
the birth of a daughter, death

of a husband, until she foundered,
struggled, and lay down in high grass
for good. Nosey, the third of six horses
to go, mourned and remembered

like the others: rides through woods,
the agreeable hills, and dry summer
creek beds, like a long breath
drawing near the end.

Broken

The mountains have shattered.
Sky milks the fields dry.
Wind tails slap the trees.
Oceans are passionately loyal.
Horses wander the oblivious night.
Footsteps mark unwanted territory.

Blue jays speak in tongues.
Windows blur clear sight.
Gardens have lost the game.
Fences tie it all together.
Unknown fish species are discovered.
Some alienate through self control.

Earth Mother lies down to rest.
How far has she come alone?
Let her crush the remaining era.
Eliminate the roaming disease.
Many parts integrate one soul.
Science knows nothing of the answers.

owl call
   horses race
      to the far field

Wolf Blood Moon

Feeding horses at night,
a falling star,
the bright moon
over pines
bordering pasture.

Like watercolors
swiped across
the dark sky
and moon, the Earth's
dusty atmosphere
quiets the sound
of sunlight.

Horses stand respectfully
waiting in fading moonlight,
nature's changes unfamiliar
yet fully accepted.
January's wolfblood moon
winks in slow motion.

Night Feeding

At the edge
    of the barn
    blackness.
Not even the backup lights
    of the car
    can be seen.

Pushing the wheelbarrow
    toward Alex,
    Lady Bug, Jack.
They nicker and wait
    for orchard grass
    and timothy hay.

Returning in the dark
    an owl sits
    on a fence post
    near my head.
The moon brushes past
    a clump
    of clouds
    to touch my shoulder.

Hope for a new day
    illuminates my path.

Full

The moon, like a solar lamp,
dim and magical, lights
the fence row

coming down the lane
from feeding the horses
their last meal of the evening.

www.ingramcontent.com/pod-product-compliance
Lightning Source LLC
Chambersburg PA
CBHW051815130726
47987CB00003B/1263